AUTISM:
A Guide *for* Families

Sherri Campbell

Halo
Publishing International

ISBN 13: 978-1-61244-320-1
Library of Congress Control Number: 2014917573

Printed in the United States of America

Halo
Publishing International
www.halopublishing.com

Published by Halo Publishing International
1100 NW Loop 410
Suite 700 - 176
San Antonio, Texas 78213
Toll Free 1-877-705-9647
www.halopublishing.com
www.holapublishing.com
e-mail: contact@halopublishing.com

This book is dedicated to my parents who taught me that all of us are created for a purpose, and all deserve the opportunities to reach our highest potential. They taught me at an early age to have compassion for others and to encourage those with challenges. I also dedicate this book to my husband, who has read every page of my work and has offered encouragement and support. Lastly, I dedicate this book to my daughters, who encouraged me to publish this information with the hope that it will be helpful to those affected by autism.

I would like to acknowledge Dr. Maribel Del Rio-Roberts and Dr. Jennifer Ries, and the professors at Nova Southeastern University who are committed to improving the lives of individuals with disabilities through the Masters of Science in Developmental Disabilities program.

Table of Contents

Preface

I have written this book to help families of children with autism. It is my belief that all children are uniquely gifted and talented with a purpose in this life. As parents, it can seem overwhelming to have a child with special needs, but as we become more knowledgeable about the conditions affecting our children, we can be proactive in assisting them to reach their highest potential.

Chapter 1:

Impact on the Family

Having a child with developmental disabilities is well-illustrated by Emily Perl Kinsley's essay entitled *Welcome to Holland:*

> I am often asked to describe the experience of raising a child with a disability — to try to help people who have not shared that unique experience to understand it, to imagine how it would feel. It's like this…
>
> When you're going to have a baby, it's like planning a fabulous vacation trip – to Italy. You buy a bunch of guide books and make your wonderful plans. The Coliseum. The Michelangelo David. The gondolas in Venice. You may learn some handy phrases in Italian. It's all very exciting.
>
> After months of eager anticipation, the day finally arrives. You pack your bags and off you go. Several hours later, the plane lands. The stewardess comes in and says, "Welcome to Holland."
>
> "Holland?!?" you say. "What do you mean, Holland?? I signed up for Italy! All my life I've dreamed of going to Italy."

But there's been a change in the flight plan. They've landed in Holland and there you must stay.

The most important thing is that they haven't taken you to a horrible, disgusting, filthy place, full of pestilence, famine, and disease. It's just a different place.

So you must go out and buy new guide books. And you must learn a whole new language. And you will meet a whole new group of people you would have never met.

It's just a different place. It's slower-paced than Italy, less flashy than Italy. But after you've been there for a while and you catch your breath, you look around…and you begin to notice that Holland has windmills…and Holland has tulips, Holland even has Rembrandts.

But everyone you know is busy coming and going from Italy…and they're all bragging about what a wonderful time they all had there. And for the rest of your life, you will say "Yes, that's where I was supposed to go. That's what I had planned."

And the pain of that will never, ever, ever, ever go away…because the loss of that dream is a very significant loss.

But…if you spend your life mourning the fact that you didn't get to Italy, you may never be free to enjoy the very special, the very lovely things…about Holland.

Parents

Parents are greatly affected when it is determined that their child has a disability, and research has indicated they may experience feelings of shock, denial, sadness, and anger (Hanson & Lynch, 2004). Although many parents mourn the loss of the child they expected, parents can view their situation not as something horrible, but instead as something different from what they had planned. As they begin the journey of parenting a child with developmental disabilities, they may be surprised at the things they are able to accomplish. Hanson & Lynch (2004) point out that families often experience increased personal growth that results in increased self-esteem and confidence as they successfully meet the challenging needs of their children. Families are also forced to develop new skills and expertise as they care for their children, and are able to assist other families dealing with similar challenges. Families are encouraged to become partners in their children's care; the family has a critical role in providing the optimal outcome for children with autism.

Research has suggested that parents may benefit from professional counseling as well as parent support groups. There are proven benefits of peer support for families of children with autism as they are able to share similar experiences with one another. Parent support groups offer support and the opportunity to share vital information about where and how to access services and obtain needed resources and support (Mandell & Salzer, 2007).

Siblings

Apart from parents, we know the entire family must adjust to changing roles when a family member is affected by developmental disability (DD). Research has indicated that there is not only an effect on parents, but siblings as well. In one particular study, parents were asked to respond to this open-ended statement: "Developmental disability in one of my children has had the following effects on the brother/sister without DD," (Williams, Piamjariyakul, Graff & Stanton, 2010). The responses to the statement were coded in a way to make it useful for interpretation. 151 parents of children with various disabilities provided more than one response, resulting in 363 tallied responses. The results showed that 61.1% of parents reported negative manifestations in siblings, 1.7% reported no effects, and 37.2% reported positive outcomes. Interestingly, these results were somewhat similar to a study by Williams et al. (2009), revealing that 74.1% of negative effects occurred in siblings of children with cancer or cystic fibrosis. Both studies identified increased risk in siblings regarding feelings of loneliness, isolation, anxiety, depression, vulnerability, anger, worry, school problems, poor peer relations, withdrawal, shyness, somatic complaints, low self-esteem, and behavior problems. Results of the Williams et al. (2010) research indicate the need for resources to help siblings of children with developmental disabilities build on their positive attributes. Family members and professionals need to be aware of the risk to siblings and work toward reducing opportunities for negative manifestations.

While it is important to monitor the impact that children with DD have upon siblings, there is little research on interventions to improve outcomes for siblings. Some data has linked sibling risk or resilience with effective parent-sibling communication about illness, family cohesion, absence of parental depression, higher levels of social support, and family resources. Parents of children with disabilities may benefit from participation in family support groups, and siblings may especially benefit from one-on-one time with their parents, potentially leading to increased feelings of family closeness, sensitivity, caregiving, personal growth, and maturation (Williams et al., 2010). Parents are encouraged to discover the areas where their "well" child excels in dealing with the affected child, and provide opportunities for positive interaction and experiences. In some situations, the siblings eventually become the primary caretakers of the family member with developmental disabilities, and it is important to honor the relationship they will have as adults by strengthening their relationships during childhood.

Grandparents

Grandparents of children with autism may experience some of the same feelings of sadness and frustration as other family members. They may experience feelings of grief for the loss of the grandchild they expected to have, and may benefit from support groups related to their grandchild's diagnosis (Hillman, 2007). Such support may be available locally and also online from organizations such as The Autism Society of America's Generations Club. Research has indicated that grandparents of children with developmental disabilities may develop a stronger relationship with their grandchildren due to increased involvement in their care (Hillman, 2007). Grandparents provide both emotional and practical support to parents of children with autism by listening, providing empathy and friendship, as well as caregiving for both respite care and work-related activities, monetary support, transportation, assistance with medical appointments, and behavioral problems, help with household chores, providing clothing and other gifts, advocacy, and service as paraprofessionals (Hillman, 2007).

Chapter 2:

Introduction to Developmental Disability

What is Autism?

Autism is a condition affecting communication skills, socialization skills, and behavior. Children with autism demonstrate delays in social interaction and play, verbal and nonverbal communication, and they demonstrate repetitive and unusual behaviors and/or interests (Brown & Percy, 2007). One of the earliest signs of autism is a lack of joint attention, which can be evident prior to the first birthday (Mundy & Newell, 2007). Joint attention is defined as the ability to share an experience, such as looking at an airplane or a picture in a book. Children with autism often do not seek the joint attention of others; they may not point to objects of interest or bring you a toy. In addition to a lack of joint attention, children with autism may exhibit poor eye contact, difficulty interacting with other children, difficulty transitioning from one activity to another, stereotypic physical behavior (rocking, spinning, lining things up, hand flapping), inappropriate attachment to objects, and sensory integration issues such as sensitivity to textures, tastes, smells and sounds. Some children with autism have feeding difficulties as a result of their sensory integration issues. Echolalia is another behavior that can be seen in children with autism and is defined as the immediate repetition of words or phrases spoken by another person, or "echo". Along with the issues related to communication, socialization and behavior, 75% of those affected by autism have intellectual disability (Osterling, Dawson & Munson, 2002).

By definition, the onset of autism occurs prior to 3 years of age. However, children are not being diagnosed as early as they could be. Data indicate that autism can be accurately diagnosed by the age of 2 (*Diagnostic and Statistical Manual of Mental Disorders*, 2000; Charman & Baird, 2002). Autism is on the rise in the United States, with the latest prevalence estimated at 1 in 68 children (Centers for Disease Control and Prevention, 2014). The increased incidence may be related to better diagnostic criteria and increasing awareness of the condition. There are ongoing studies attempting to establish a link between genetic and environmental factors as contributors to the condition, but until we isolate the cause, we will be unable to prevent its occurrence (Irva Hertz-Piccioto, 2006). What we can do is provide opportunities for children and adults with autism to reach their highest potential.

Autism was first described by Leo Tanner in 1943. It is a condition that has been misunderstood, and is one that continues to intrigue many of us. Early on, autism was felt to be related to a deficit in the maternal bond; however, with much more study on the condition, it has been determined to be a behaviorally defined syndrome (Brown & Percy, 2009). Until recently, most professionals used the definition found in the Diagnostic and Statistical Manual of Mental Disorders, Fourth Edition (DSM-IV), which includes autism as one of five disorders under the general category of pervasive developmental disorders. The other disorders include Asperger's Syndrome, Pervasive Developmental Disorder-Not Otherwise Specified (PDD-NOS), and two degenerative disorders: Rett Syndrome and Childhood Disintegrative Disorder. In 2013, the American Psychological Association published the 5th edition of the DSM, which eliminates the condition known as Asperger's

Syndrome and uses the term Autism Spectrum Disorder (ASD) for both autism and Asperger's Syndrome. In the DSM-V, Autism Spectrum Disorder is characterized as occurring with or without language impairment, with or without cognitive impairment, and/or associated with other medical or environmental conditions. The DSM-V also provides categories for individuals with autism based on the severity of the condition, with level 1 "requiring support"; level 2 "requiring substantial support"; and level 3 "requiring very substantial support". Autism is a lifelong condition, occurring more in boys than girls. With appropriate support and intervention from the time of diagnosis into adulthood, many of those affected can have a better quality of life.

What is Asperger's Syndrome?

Asperger's Syndrome is similar to autism, and is one of the disorders included in the DSM-IV category of autism spectrum disorders. Individuals affected by Asperger's Syndrome usually do not have delays in speech and language, and demonstrate better communication skills and cognitive capacities than those with autism (Shtayermman, 2007). Asperger's Syndrome is sometimes referred to as "high-functioning autism", but there is some debate about the accuracy of this term and whether or not high-functioning autism is a separate and distinct clinical entity from Asperger's Syndrome (Volkmar & Klin, 2001). With the revision of the DSM-V, individuals formerly considered to have Asperger's Syndrome would be referred to as having ASD without intellectual or language impairment. Most individuals formerly considered to have had Asperger's Syndrome would fall under severity level 1.

Chapter 3:

Early Intervention Services for Children with Autism

What is early intervention?

Early intervention services have been proven to be beneficial in achieving better outcomes for individuals with autism (Dawson, 2008). Early intervention services, as described by the National Center for Children with Disabilities at nichcy.org, are services that help babies and toddlers with developmental delays or disabilities, and focus on helping them learn the basic skills that typically develop during the first three years of life (National Dissemination Center for Children with Disabilities, n.d.). Examples of services provided by early intervention include:

- Assistive technology: (Devices such as walkers and wheelchairs, as well as hardware and software, that help disabled individuals access computers or other information technologies.)
- Audiology
- Speech and Language Services
- Counseling and Family Training
- Medical Services

- Nursing Services
- Nutrition Services
- Occupational Therapy
- Physical Therapy
- Psychological Services

What are the benefits of early intervention?

Children with autism who receive services have been found to score higher on IQ tests (Dawson, 2008; Dawson, 2009). The benefits of early intervention have been well-known for many years, and in the United States, all children with developmental disabilities, including autism, are entitled by law to receive free and appropriate educational services (Guralnick, 1998; Gardner & Chapman, 1993). Early identification of developmental disability allows for early intervention services to begin, and research indicates that the earlier intervention begins, the better the outcome (Boyd, Odom, Humphreys & Sam, 2010).

There is evidence that early behavioral intervention can significantly impact the long-term prognosis for children with autism (Osterling, Dawson & Munson, 2002). The importance of early intervention has been increasingly recognized, as many studies have found that children with autism spectrum disorders who receive services prior to 48 months of age make greater improvements than those who enter programs after 48 months of age (Corsello, 2005). Results from a study by Turner, Stone, Pozdol, and Coonrod (2006) have also provided evidence indicating the positive effects of early intervention for children who received additional hours of speech and language therapy between 2 and 3 years of age. At the follow-up evaluation, some of the participating children no longer met the diagnostic criteria for autism. After completing a review of early intensive behavioral intervention programs for children with autism that confirmed increased IQ levels following early intervention, Eldevik et al. (2009) state that, "Early Intensive Behavioral Intervention should be an intervention of choice for children with autism."

Legal Rights Related to Early Intervention

Prior to the 1970's, children with disabilities were often denied the opportunity for education. However, the Education for all Handicapped Children Act of 1975 required that all children with disabilities be provided a free and appropriate public education (Hanson & Lynch, 2004). In 1986, an amendment to the 1975 law provided for early intervention services for children with developmental disabilities. There have been several additional amendments to the initial law that strengthened early intervention services, and in 1990, the name of the law was changed to the Individuals with Disabilities Education Act (IDEA), to which amendments were made in 1997.

The IDEA Early Intervention program places primary emphasis on strengthening the ability of parents to promote their children's learning and development. IDEA outlines six principles that provide the framework for educational policies and services for children with disabilities and their families:

- Free and appropriate public education
- Appropriate evaluation
- Development of individualized education programs
- Education provided in the least restrictive environment
- Parent and student participation in decision making
- Procedural safeguards to protect the rights of parents and their child with a disability

Requirements were also added to provide assistance to

eligible students with transition into post-secondary education following graduation, vocational training, supported employment, continuing education, and employment and/or community living (Hanson & Lynch, 2004).

Established in 1986, the Early Intervention Program for Infants and Toddlers with Disabilities, or Part C of the IDEA, provides for early intervention services for children from birth to 3 years of age. Part C defines legal rights to early intervention, defining what constitutes developmental delay, rules for completing developmental evaluation, and mandating services for those who are eligible (Hanson & Lynch, 2004). Part B is the section of IDEA outlining services for children from 3 to 5 years of age (Hanson & Lynch, 2004). The definitions of Parts B and C services vary somewhat from state to state, and the funding is provided from both state and federal grants (National Dissemination Center for Children with Disabilities, n.d.).

Funding for Early Intervention Services

Intervention services for children with autism may be accessed through different funding sources, including Part C federal and state grants and private insurance. Unfortunately, there has been much variability in the type and intensity of Part C services offered from state to state. In the National Early Intervention Longitudinal Study, Hebbler et al. (2007) reported that the median number of service hours provided to infants and toddlers with developmental delays during the first 6 months of service was 1.5 hours/week. This intensity is far less than the recommended 25 hours of intensive intervention per week as proposed by the National Academy of Sciences Committee on Educating Children with Autism (Boyd et al., 2010). Some states have adopted programs within the Medicaid system to allow for waivers to assist in obtaining funding for early intervention services specifically for children with autism

(Boyd et al., 2010). Families would need to work with their local early intervention programs to determine what funding is available for their child.

Types of Early Intervention Services

The administration of early intervention services for children with developmental disabilities varies greatly. Early intervention services for children have historically been administered at a local facility by therapists or teachers utilizing a service-based model, with the philosophy that more time face-to-face with the child would provide better outcomes. However, this has not been supported by recent research (Odom, Horner, Snell & Blacher, 2007). More effective practices have been demonstrated in programs that operate with a functional perspective in a natural environment such as the child's home or daycare. In these settings, individualized goals are pursued that help each child gain the skills he/she needs to become more independent and successful within his/her physical and social environment. These programs work toward outcomes that provide skills that allow the child to participate more fully in a variety of community settings (Odom, et al., 2007).

Early intervention that is known to positively affect the learning and development of young children with disabilities has been found to include four common practices: 1) response-contingent child learning; 2) parent responsiveness to child behavior; 3) everyday natural learning opportunities; and 4) capacity-building, help-giving practices (Odom et al., 2007).

> **Response-contingent child learning** occurs when a child produces a behavior that results in an interesting consequence that reinforces the original behavior, as found in the relationship between what he/she does and what happens in response. Research has indicated that achievement is pleasurable, and that social and episodic reinforcers are more

desirable, making this a useful early intervention practice for working with children with developmental disabilities.

Parent responsiveness to child behavior is very important in achieving positive outcomes for children with developmental disabilities (Odom et al., 2007). Children who realize their parents are nurturing and dependable have the advantage of having an optimal environment for learning and development. Parents who share in their child's efforts and successes, and encourage and support them, provide opportunities for better outcomes for their children with developmental disabilities (Odom et al., 2007).

Everyday natural learning opportunities are those that occur in the context of family and community life. Preschoolers participate in 40-50 different kinds of activities on a regular basis, but children with developmental disabilities participate in about half as many activities. This is felt to be related to parents' lack of understanding regarding the value of everyday learning opportunities (Odom et al., 2007). Odom et al. (2007) have also noted that parental use of everyday activities as a source of natural learning opportunities is associated with positive outcome measures.

Capacity-building, help-giving practices are those that include efforts of early intervention practitioners to support and encourage parents, and ideally result in increased competence and confidence in parents and children with disabilities.

While early intervention for children with autism has resulted in significant improvement in cognition, language, and the ability to function in school (Brown & Percy, 2009), many different practices have been utilized to administer services. No matter the practice, all education plans should be individualized; each child with the condition has a unique presentation with varied strengths and weaknesses. The skills targeted by early intervention programs should be functional, usable across settings, observable and measurable, and should benefit the child as part of their natural daily environment (Odom et al., 2007). There are several critical factors to consider when planning for early intervention services to address autism. The intervention should promote active engagement of the child with others, should include Applied Behavioral Analysis (ABA) principles, and should consider the family's perspective (Brown & Percy, 2009). Brown and Percy (2009) have noted that successful programs have had the following common features:

- The children began receiving services between 2 and 4 years of age.Services were intensive, often consisting of 20-40 hours/week during the first two years.
- Structured behavioral teaching principles were utilized.
- The programs were comprehensive.
- The programs were individualized.
- Highly trained staff and parents were involved in the treatment.
- Inclusion with typically developing peers was implemented.

Focused-Based Interventions

Focused-based interventions are evidence-based practices that have proven to be effective in helping children with autism (Boyd et al., 2010). They incorporate helpful techniques for modifying behavior as well as attaining communication skills (Odom et al., 2007). In addition to behavioral therapies, early intervention services to establish functional communication also play a large role in minimizing the lifelong effects of young children with autism (Odom et al., 2007). Odom et al. (2007) describe differential reinforcement, discrete-trial training, naturalistic behavioral interventions, pivotal-response training, peer-mediated interventions, positive behavior support, and self-management as those interventions that are well-established.

- **Differential reinforcement** is when an adult provides rewards for desired behavior.
- **Discrete-trial training** is a highly-focused, teaching trial practice where an adult and child engage in individual teaching sessions that provide reinforcement on a predetermined schedule.
- **Naturalistic behavioral interventions** are conducted during a child's ongoing routine and in his/her natural environment that has been arranged to allow the child to initiate the skills to be learned, and includes reinforcement for the desired behavior.
- **Pivotal response training** is based on the theory that the motivation to respond to complex stimuli is a core deficit in autism, and focuses on the pivotal behaviors of responsiveness to multiple cues, self-management, and self-initiation of social interaction.
- **Peer-mediated interventions** focus on social or communicative behaviors utilizing peers who have been taught to initiate or direct specific types of social behaviors that encourage use of skills or targeted behaviors.
- **Positive behavior support (PBS)** includes interventions such as functional behavior assessment, with emphasis on factors that lead to unacceptable behavior and modifications in the environment to reduce them. Individuals can benefit from functional communication training insofar as it helps them communicate the need for a break to help them avoid becoming so frustrated that they begin to exhibit unacceptable behavior. PBS has been implemented

successfully for children with autism who have serious problem behaviors.

- **Self-management** has been successful with older children with autism, as adults directly teach them to monitor, record, and/or reinforce their use of a desired behavior or skill.

Examples of Successful Early Intervention Programs

As children with autism are identified at earlier ages, specific early intervention programs for young children with autism have been created. There are several comprehensive programs that have demonstrated remarkable progress in serving toddlers, in the birth to age 3 category (Odom et al., 2007). Most comprehensive models are center-based, and all emphasize family involvement, and parent education and training. The **Walden Toddler Program** utilizes incidental teaching, a type of ABA using behavioral principles within a natural learning environment, with heavy emphasis on parental involvement and social inclusion. The **Children's Toddler School** is similar to the Walden Toddler Program, but includes additional behavioral and nonverbal communication intervention techniques taking place in inclusive settings. An additional program for toddlers with autism is the **Project DATA Program**, which provides an inclusive early childhood program, extended instruction time, technical and social support for families, coordination of family-negotiated services, and transition. The **Early Start Denver Model** and the **Early Social Interaction Project** are successful programs where parents learn to implement interventions in their homes to promote their toddler's development (Boyd et al., 2010).

Individualized Family Service Plans (IFSPs)

The educational plan developed for implementing IDEA Part C early intervention services is called the IFSP, or Individualized Family Service Plan (National Dissemination Center for Children with Disabilities, n.d.). The IFSP is a written document outlining services that the child and family will receive. It is guided by the principle that the family is a child's greatest resource, and a child's needs are closely tied to the needs of his/her family (National Dissemination Center for Children with Disabilities, n.d.). Parents are major contributors to the development of this plan, and other team members may include medical professionals, therapists, child development specialists, and social workers. IFSPs include:

- Information regarding the child's current physical, cognitive, communicative, social/emotional, and adaptive development levels and needs.
- Family information such as family resources, priorities, and family concerns.
- Services the child will receive along with the duration, location, and times and days they will be provided. Services are generally facilitated in the natural environment of the child, such as the home or daycare, which is also documented.
- Funding sources, along with the contact information and name of the primary service coordinator.
- The IFSP must be reviewed every six months and updated once per year. Transition into other programs is also addressed, and as the child progresses from early intervention programs into school based programs, the IFSP will outline the requirements necessary to make those changes, allowing for minimal interruption in services (National Dissemination Center for Children with Disabilities, n.d.).

Accessing Local Early Intervention Programs

In the United States, a parent who is concerned that their child may have developmental delays can begin to access early intervention services even if no diagnosis has been made (National Dissemination Center for Children with Disabilities, n.d.). Parents can obtain specific information regarding each state's early intervention services online, from the Department of Education. In the state of Florida, parents are encouraged to call their local intake center for early interventions services, the Florida Diagnostic and Learning Resource Center (FDLRS), and ask for an evaluation. Children under 3 years of age will be referred to the Early Steps Program, and children over 3 will be referred to the Pre-K Exceptional Student Education Program. They will be assigned a primary service coordinator who will schedule a developmental screen and/or evaluation. Some children will be eligible for services without evaluation if they have a physical or mental condition that qualifies them for an exception. Based on the findings from the screening or evaluation, an initial assessment will be completed to identify the unique needs and early intervention services to be provided, and the IFSP will be completed. Services will be initiated and state and federal grants will assure that no cost will be placed on the family (National Dissemination Center for Children with Disabilities, n.d.).

Family Resources for Early Intervention

A good source of information and support for families is **Autism Speaks**. At www.autismspeaks.org, families can obtain toolkits on many topics related to autism, such as how to navigate the first 100 days following an autism diagnosis. A variety of resources are also available on the site.

For parents of children with feeding difficulties, valuable information is available from **Feeding Matters** at www.feedingmatters.org. This organization is committed to improving pediatric feeding struggles and provides support and information for families and medical professionals. **The American Speech-Language Hearing Association** at www.asha.org is another source of information about feeding disorders that may be beneficial to parents and professionals. **The National Foundation of Swallowing Disorders** at www.swallowingdisorderfoundation.com also provides information and support to those affected by feeding difficulties.

The following resources are examples of state-specific assistance. Families are encouraged to seek out such resources in their own areas. Families of children with autism in the Lee County, Florida area can contact the Center for Autism and Related Disabilities Program (CARD), located at Florida Gulf Coast University. This program is a community outreach program from the University of South Florida and is designed to provide information, consultation, instruction, and coaching for families and children affected by autism. On their website, http://card-usf.fmhi.usf.edu, families can obtain information and see videos providing helpful information regarding autism. This organization also provides a local support group for families affected by autism, and provides services to professionals through a training and assistance model.

At the **Golisano Children's Hospital of Southwest Florida**, an autism navigator position is being created to assist families of children diagnosed with autism. The navigator would be available following diagnosis and would assist the family in obtaining early intervention services, medical treatment, and funding.

Chapter 4:

Educational Opportunities for Children with Autism

History of Educational Opportunities for Children with Autism

Children with autism and developmental disabilities have historically been separated from their families and communities, and until the mid-1900's, they were not provided with any opportunity for education (Brown & Percy, 2007). Following World War II, efforts were made in the areas of human rights and social equality, and parents of children with disabilities began to advocate strongly for educational and social services for their children. It was not until 1973 that legislation was passed recognizing the rights of persons with disabilities in the form of Section 504 of the Rehabilitation Act of 1973 (PL-93-112), prohibiting discrimination of people with disabilities who participate in any program or activity receiving federal funding (Brown & Percy, 2007). It was two years later that the Education for All Handicapped Children Act (EHA) of 1975 (PL-94-142) was created, providing for an appropriate and free public education for all children, including those with disabilities (Odom et al., 2007).

Since that time, there has been much debate about the definition of appropriate education for children with disabilities, and most recently, the trend has been toward inclusive education for all children. Inclusion is the process of jointly teaching children with and without disabilities together in the same classroom, and if necessary, bringing support services to the children instead of removing them to obtain services (Brown & Percy, 2007). Inclusive education represents a systematic approach to school reform that allows general education and special education services to work together to create a shared educational agenda and a fully integrated and coordinated system of educational services (Odom et al., 2007). Research has shown that inclusive education results in improved academic skills and social outcomes for students with developmental disabilities when compared with those in separate special education settings (Logan & Keefe, 1997).

Early Legislation

In developed countries it is now widely accepted that all children, including those with disabilities, will attend school throughout their childhood years (Brown & Percy, 2007). The EHA mentioned above provides for a free, appropriate education in the least restrictive environment for all students with disabilities, and should be "designed to meet the unique needs of a handicapped child, including classroom instruction, home instruction and instruction in hospitals and institutions," (Odom et al., 2007; Brown & Percy, 2007).

There has been much debate regarding provision of education in the least restrictive environment, as there is a lack of clarity as to what constitutes a least restrictive environment (Howard, 2004). The law specifies that services should be provided to the maximum extent possible in environments where children with disabilities are educated with children without disabilities. Furthermore, they should only be removed from such environment if education cannot be achieved adequately in the general education environment, even if supplemental aids or services are required (Odom et al., 2007).

Inclusive Education

The term "inclusion" was first discussed in the literature in 1990, and according to Odom et al. (2007), it occurs when students with disabilities "attend their home schools and receive educational services through full-time placement in chronologically age appropriate general education classes within the context of the core curriculum and general class activities and in integrated community settings." Students with disabilities who are enrolled in general education classrooms are members of that classroom, and are viewed as kids who are part of the natural school and the classroom to which they belong, who happen to have a disability (Odom et al., 2007). Kochhar, West, and Taymans (2000) identify six key components of inclusive education:

- Children with disabilities attend neighborhood schools.
- Schools and classrooms reflect proportions of children with disabilities found in the general population.
- No student is excluded because of their disability (zero-rejection philosophy).
- Students with disabilities are placed in classes with peers of the same age.
- Students with and without disabilities take part in cooperative learning and peer instruction.
- Needed special education resources, including personnel, are available within the general education classroom.

Inclusive Education Legislation

Initially, there was movement toward "integration," or providing special education classrooms for children with disabilities in neighborhood schools. This movement was followed by "mainstreaming," in which children with disabilities were taught primarily in the special education classrooms, but visited the general education classrooms for some opportunities with typically developing children (Odom et al., 2007).

Then in the 1980's, Madeleine Will, who served as Assistant Secretary for the Office of Special Education and Rehabilitation Services, introduced the Regular Education Initiative (REI). REI encouraged general education and special education partnerships based on research by Margaret Wang, Herbert Wahlberg, and Maynard Reynolds that reported positive outcomes for students with mild disabilities in general education classrooms. There have been several amendments to the initial REI, and in 1990 the name of the law was changed to the Individuals with Disabilities Education Act (IDEA).

IDEA provided a major shift toward alignment of special education services with broader educational reforms, reaffirming the idea that students with disabilities should be educated in general education classrooms, have access to general education curricula, and be included in state and local district assessments (Odom et al., 2007). Provision was also made for coordinated implementation of IDEA and other school improvement acts, such as Title I Schoolwide Programs, to promote unified educational services. This shift in policy for students receiving special education services was also reflected in the newly reauthorized IDEA of 2004, renamed the Individuals with Disabilities Education Improvement Act. In 2001, President Bush created the No Child Left Behind Act (NCLB), identifying all children in public school as general education students, and promoting the use of "whole school" approaches (such as evidence-based reading programs, positive behavior interventions, and early intervention services) in an effort to reduce referrals for special education services (Odom et al., 2007). NCLB also mandates statewide assessments annually for all children in grades three through eight, including those with disabilities, to ensure that students are making progress (Odom et al., 2007).

The REI was met with resistance from those in the field of special education, but it was the first U.S. Department of Education policy to address services provided through separate, categorical placements, and provided incentive for research in the area of inclusive education. Parents and professionals argued that students with disabilities should not be segregated and should have access to typically developing children, allowing for friendships with peers in the general education classroom (Odom et al., 2007).

Challenges Faced by Children with Autism in the Classroom

It is important to note that there is much variation in the presentation of features associated with autism, and children with autism require very individualized plans to meet their educational needs. Winzer (2002) noted problems with grouping children for instruction, as many children who are classified, or labeled, in the same way have very different instructional needs. Most students with autism struggle with skills needed to be successful in the general education setting. Smith (2012) has identified five specific challenges faced by children with autism in the classroom:

1. Engaging in goal-directed, future oriented behaviors such as planning and sustaining attention to relevant stimuli
2. Thinking flexibility and solving problems
3. Organizing multiple pieces of information simultaneously

to form concepts;

4. Remembering information from past personal experience and applying that information to new situations; and
5. Self-monitoring and management of behavior.

Individualized Education Plans (IEPs)

Individualized planning is critical to address the unique needs of each child with disabilities (Hanson & Lynch, 2004). School-aged children with autism can benefit from a thorough psychoeducational assessment to obtain data needed to identify individual curricular, instructional, and behavioral supports required to achieve success in the general education classroom (Smith, 2012). Following assessment, Individualized Education Plans (IEPs) are created and specify what needs to be taught, what supports are needed, and what evaluation will be used to monitor progress (Brown & Percy, 2007). Decisions for placement can be made by a team of school personnel and parents to determine which environment can best support the educational goals and objectives of the individual student (Brown & Percy, 2007). In the United States, IDEA requires all children with disabilities to have an IEP, which consists of written statements including:

- The child's present level of performance
- Measureable annual goals and objectives to meet the child's educational needs
- Special education and related services, supplementary aids and services, and program modifications or supports needed to enable the child to meet educational goals and participate with other children
- An explanation of the extent, if any, to which the child will not be involved in a general education classroom

- Any necessary modification in the administration of the state or school district assessments of student achievement in order for the child to participate
- The date to begin services, and the frequency, location, and duration of services and modifications
- Identification of the system for measuring the child's progress toward goals set forth by the IEP team, which will consist of the child's parents, general education teacher, special education teacher, representatives of local education agencies, and others who may have knowledge of the child or expertise regarding the child (Hanson & Lynch, 2004)

Inclusive Education Research

Placement decisions have been controversial in special education, as there are philosophical differences about what is best for students with special needs. There has been conflicting research regarding what is best for these students, but the overall trend in more developed countries is for placement in general education classrooms in neighborhood schools, unless a better alternative is found (Brown & Percy, 2007). A number of studies have resulted in encouraging findings for some children with autism in some inclusive classrooms (Harrower & Dunlap, 2001). Some researchers believe that inclusion for children with autism is important for educational and social success. However, inclusion can only work well if the education system is designed to encourage and support its success (Harrower & Dunlap, 2001).

Research in the area of inclusive education is difficult to conduct. There have been several studies completed using small sample sizes, but there is much more research still needed. Sansosti & Sansosti (2012) studied inclusion for students with high-functioning autism spectrum disorders and found that multiple complex factors were critical in determining success. They determined that factors to be considered when making a placement decision include individual student needs, educational goals, available supports, best practice approaches to instruction, and the potential impact of introducing a student with significant instructional supports and/or behavioral supports into a general education classroom. In that study, educators felt that inclusion was a valuable practice that could yield positive results — not only for students with high-functioning autism, but also for their general education peers and teachers. Positive outcomes have included accelerated skill development of students with high functioning autism through engagement in challenging academic tasks and new social situations, and it was felt the entire class benefitted from the implementation of behavioral supports and teaching of social skills (Sansosti & Sansosti, 2012).

Additional studies of children with high-functioning autism in general education classrooms were performed by Dahle (2003), who found students had increased levels of engagement and social interaction; and Chamberlain, Kasari & Rotheram-Fuller (2007), who noted that children had larger networks of friends, and were selected to be included in peer activities at the same frequency as students without disabilities (Sansosti & Sansosti, 2012). Some have argued that typically developing students may suffer when students with disabilities are placed in the general education classroom, but studies have shown no difference in the progress of children without disabilities in an inclusive setting alongside children with disabilities (Odom, et al., 2007).

Odom et al. (2007) states that there is continued opposition to inclusive school reform due to the lack of "buy in" from the general education community and continued opposition to inclusive education policy and practices within the special education community. Tomsho (2007), as cited by Smith (2012), states, "There are skeptics who worry that the real motives for focusing on the least restrictive environment are sometimes more pecuniary than principled: Inclusive placements tend to be cheaper than self-contained classrooms." For these reasons, the number of children with disabilities attending general education classrooms is limited but on the increase. Sansosti and Sansosti (2012) report participation of students with autism in the general education classroom for more than 80% of the day —increased from 9% in 1992-1993 to 31% in 2005-2006.

Strategies for Success in the Inclusive Education Classroom

Schools need to have experts in autism and behavior analysis readily available in inclusive classrooms, and teachers need adequate resources and social support in order to be successful (Harrower & Dunlap, 2001). Several strategies specific to children with autism have been beneficial in the general education classroom. Some are considered "antecedent" procedures, as they are designed to prevent and reduce challenging behaviors. Strategies that have been proven to be successful in educating children with autism include:

- **Priming, or prepractice,** which allows for previewing information or activities that a child is likely to have difficulty with before he/she engages in that activity (Harrower & Dunlap, 2001).
- **Prompt delivery** provides prompts, or signals, before a school transition, allowing for students to make easier transitions from one activity to another (Harrower & Dunlap, 2001).
- **Picture schedules** can serve as effective cues indicating upcoming changes, increasing predictability, and helping

with transitions (Harrower & Dunlap, 2001).

- **Delayed contingencies, or rewards**, is another strategy that has proven successful in assisting children with autism to be independent in the classroom. Research has indicated that children with autism experience improved behavior and productivity with an unpredictable use of supervision, when compared with predictable supervision (Harrower & Dunlap, 2001).
- **Self-management** strategies shift the responsibility for behavior from the teacher to the student. Children are taught the difference between appropriate and inappropriate behavior, to evaluate and monitor their own behavior, and to reinforce their own behavior when prespecified criteria are met (Harrower & Dunlap, 2001).
- **Peer-mediated interventions** reduce the need for one-to-one adult attention by utilizing peers to support the academic function of students with autism (Harrower & Dunlap, 2001).
- **Peer tutoring** is another effective strategy, allowing for the pairing of two students to work together, whereby one student provides instruction, assistance and feedback to the other (Harrower & Dunlap, 2001).
- **Utilizing peer supports**, similar to peer tutoring, where a typically developing student serves as a source of peer support (Harrower & Dunlap, 2001).
- **Cooperative learning** has also proven beneficial when teaching social and academic skills to children with autism and typically developing peers in integrated group settings, and has been proven to increase the frequency, quality, and duration of social interactions (Harrower & Dunlap, 2001).
- **Professional teaming** is a strategy in which professionals

work as a team to support student's participation. It utilizes parents, special and gifted teachers, and instructional assistants (Odom, et al., 2007).

- **Positive behavior support** (PBS) is a well-established process of functional behavioral assessment and assessment-based interventions that has been implemented effectively with a wide range of students across diverse educational and community environments (Sailor, Dunlap, Sugai & Horner, 2009). One example of PBS is "Prevent-Teach-Reinforce" (PTR). This support is designed for classroom settings to meet the need for a standardized model of functional-based behavioral interventions for students with severe behavior problems. Students who received PTR intervention demonstrated significantly higher improvements in social skills, behavior, and academic engagement (Crosland & Dunlap, 2012).

Chapter 5:

Transitioning from School to Adult Life

Transition is defined as passage from one state, stage, subject, or place to another (*Webster's Dictionary for Students*, 2003). Transition as it pertains to those with developmental disabilities refers to the changes that take place when children enter the school system from early intervention programs, and when students move from secondary school to adult life. Individuals with autism spectrum disorders have much difficulty with transitions and require preparation if they are to be successful (VanBergeijk, Klin & Volkmar, 2008). A smooth transition from school life to adult life is a major component in successful inclusion of young adults into community life (Brown & Percy, 2007).

The Florida Administrative Code in Rule 6A-6.03411 defines transition services as a "coordinated set of activities for a student with a disability that is designed to be within a result-oriented process, that is focused on improving the academic and functional achievement of the student with a disability to facilitate movement from school to post-school activities, including postsecondary education, vocational education, integrated employment (including supported employment), continuing and adult education, adult services, independent living, or community participation; and is based on the individual student's needs, taking into account the student strengths, preferences and interests," (Roberts-Dahm, 2005). Transition planning is the process by which students, families and educators develop plans and identify supports and services that will promote success during these important stages in the life of an individual with developmental disabilities (Odom et al., 2007). There is much variation in the presentation of features associated with autism, and it is very important to develop individualized plans to assist autistic individuals with transition.

Transition Planning

Transition planning should focus on dreams and aspirations that young people have for the future (Roberts-Dahm, 2005). Planning should begin no later than the age of 14 to allow for sufficient time to obtain and utilize services and supports that will enable a successful move into adult life (Roberts-Dahm, 2005). It is mandated by the Individuals with Disabilities Education Act of 1990 and the amendments of 1997 and 2004, that schools identify needed in-school and post-school transition services for all youth with disabilities beginning at age 16 or younger. These services are intended to prepare students for employment and independent living (Odom et al., 2007).

Most students with autism will have an Individualized Educational Plan (IEP) in place during their educational years, which provides information on their abilities, measurable goals and objectives, and special educational services and supports (Hanson & Lynch, 2004). It is important to incorporate transition planning into the IEP and to include all members of the IEP team, such as the student, family, school staff, agency staff and others that may be of help in achieving the student's goals. During the IEP meetings, it is important that the student identifies his/her goals for adult life, and families can prepare their students by exploring options for the future prior to the transition meeting. It is important to remember, however, that changes can be made to the plan as needed (Roberts-Dahm, 2005).

Diploma Options

As students and their families identify goals for the future, it is important to consider options available for obtaining a high school diploma, as this decision may impact the opportunities available following graduation. Most states offer several diploma options. There are three diploma options available in the state of Florida, and the IEP team makes an initial diploma decision during the young person's eighth grade year or during the school year when they turn 14, whichever comes first (Roberts-Dahm, 2005). It is important to note that this decision can be changed at any time in the future through an IEP meeting.

The diploma options available include a **Standard Diploma; Special Diploma, Option 1; or Special Diploma, Option 2**. Students with disabilities may need additional time to obtain the diploma of their choice, and they have the option to remain in school until age 22. If they do not meet the requirements to obtain a Standard or Special Diploma, they may be awarded a regular or special certificate of completion (Roberts-Dahm, 2005).

> **A Standard Diploma** is the type of diploma earned by most students and is awarded when a student earns the required amount of credits in high school, maintains a 2.0 grade point average, and passes the Florida Comprehensive Assessment Test (FCAT) and FCAT 2.0. There are provisions for students with disabilities to waive the FCAT testing, and if certain criteria are met, the student can be awarded a Standard Diploma with FCAT waiver and End-of-Course Assessment Waivers.
>
> **Special Diploma, Option 1** is available to students who have been identified as having intellectual disability, autism spectrum disorder, language impairment, orthopedic

impairment, health impairment, traumatic brain injury, emotional or behavioral disability, or specific learning disability. Students must earn the minimum number of credits required by their school districts to earn the Special Diploma, Option 1.

Special Diploma, Option 2 is available to students who complete an individually designed training plan that includes employment and community living skills. Students must be employed at or above minimum wage salaries for a least one semester, demonstrate mastery of competencies at his/her job, and meet school district requirements to be eligible for a Special Diploma, Option 2.

For students who complete the required courses but are unable to meet the requirement for either of the diplomas, there is the option to obtain a Certificate of Completion. One additional option for those who have not earned a Standard Diploma has been to try to pass the Tests of General Educational Development (GED), which has recently undergone revision and has been renamed the Florida High School Performance-Based Diploma (Roberts-Dahm, 2005).

It is recommended that young people with developmental disabilities should work toward obtaining a Standard Diploma if possible, as colleges, universities, and branches of the military usually do not accept Special Diplomas, which could result in limited options for post-school life (Roberts-Dahm, 2005).

Post-Secondary Education

The increasing prevalence of autism in the United States in the last two decades has presented challenges to our educational system. Fombonne (2005) estimated that there were between 284,000 and 486,000 individuals with pervasive developmental disorder under the age of 20. VanBergeijk,

Klin and Volkmar (2008) point out the overwhelming majority of those with pervasive developmental disorder have milder forms of autism, stating that the incidence of Asperger's Syndrome is double the number of those affected by classic autism. Individuals affected by Asperger's Syndrome (now described as "autism without language or intellectual impairment", American Psychiatric Association, 2013) demonstrate significant and limiting interpersonal deficits, similar to those with classic autism; however, they may demonstrate cognitive abilities similar to neurotypical or gifted individuals (Barnhill, Hagiwara, Myles & Simpson, 2000). Students with Asperger's Syndrome often have excellent vocabularies but have difficulty with semantics and pragmatics of speech, making conversation difficult (VanBergeijk et al., 2008).

Many individuals with autism spectrum disorder are intellectually capable of attaining a college education; however, they may require academic and supportive accommodations to assist them in academics as well as independent living (VanBergeijk et al., 2008). Results from a study by Taylor and Seltzer (2010) indicated that nearly 50% of the participants with autistic spectrum disorders without intellectual disability (defined as having an IQ above 70) were pursuing a post-secondary educational degree.

VanBergeijk et al. (2008) have outlined specific interventions and supports that may be helpful for individuals with autism whose goals include obtaining a college education. The transition plan as outlined in the IEP should include exposure to college curriculum while the student is still in high school. Local community college classes can provide such exposure to the demands of the college environment. Courses selected should be chosen by the students in his/her area of strength to best allow for success. Benefits of this intervention may also include decreased future stress levels by reducing the number of courses the student will have to take each semester (VanBergeijk et al., 2008).

It is also recommended that the student and family consider the differences between small colleges and large universities when determining the best fit for post-secondary education. Small colleges offer the advantage of smaller classrooms, familiarity, and personalized learning environments, whereas large universities offer students with autism the possibility of finding their social and vocational "niche" (VanBergeijk et al., 2008). It is also important to determine the level of support offered to students with disabilities at different institutions. This determination can be made by examining the college or university's Office of Student Disabilities (OSD) statistics to determine the number of students with disabilities currently attending. Students with disabilities will need to register with the university's OSD to be eligible to receive classroom accommodations, and in accordance with the ADA, to receive test-taking accommodations that may be necessary for success (VanBergeijk et al., 2008). Universities need to be able to provide support services in the areas of social skills groups, psycho-educational groups, directive counseling, vocational training and life coaching in order to best serve students with autism spectrum disorders (VanBergeijk et al., 2008).

Research Regarding Outcomes

Research regarding quality of life outcomes for adult individuals with autism has been challenging. Researchers evaluate outcomes for individuals with disabilities, using quality of life indicators in areas such as material well-being, emotional well-being, physical well-being, self-determination, rights, social inclusion, interpersonal relationships and personal development (Odom et al., 2007). There are two national databases that monitor outcomes for youth with disabilities: The National Longitudinal Transition Study (NLTS) and (NTLS2); and the National Organization on Disability (NOD) (Odom et al., 2007). Both databases have indicated poor outcomes for adults with disabilities in almost all domains, especially in the areas of material well-being and personal development.

Individuals with disabilities are less likely to be employed, enrolled in post-secondary education, live independently, or own a home (Odom et al., 2007). They are more likely to live in poverty and worry about their futures, and are less likely to have friends and social activities. Some research has noted that those with more severe disabilities experience poorer outcomes than those considered to have more mild disabilities (Odom et al., 2007). During their school years, individuals with autism spectrum disorders generally have a gradual reduction in severity of autism-related symptoms and maladaptive behaviors, but following graduation, this improvement slows (Taylor & Seltzer, 2010). One study also found that performance IQ generally declines with age while verbal IQ increases (Howlin, Goode, Hutton & Rutter, 2004). Some researchers indicate that this decline in IQ and slowed improvement may be related to a lack of stimulating adult occupations and day activities following completion of secondary education (Taylor & Seltzer, 2010).

The knowledge obtained from these studies may seem overwhelming for families, but it can be used to help identify opportunities that allow our children with autism identify strengths and work toward obtaining skills that will lead to employment, independent living, and development of friendships, resulting in a better quality of life.

Employment

Lack of employment has a dramatic effect on quality of life. When individuals are employed, they earn discretionary income that allows them the ability to choose where they live, who they live with, and how they spend their money (Odom et al., 2007). Having a place of employment provides a social network and the opportunity to have friends. Unfortunately, there have been few opportunities for individuals with disabilities in the past. In the 1960's, little was expected of those with disabilities, and most work opportunities revolved around learning activities of daily living in segregated settings. In the 1970's, interventions were developed to assist those with disabilities in community job settings instead of segregated and sheltered workshops. In the 1980's, strategies were developed to provide employment supports in integrated jobs instead of segregated vocational settings, and in the 1990's research revealed the capacity of coworkers and supervisors to provide "natural supports" in individualized work settings. Researchers also realized that people with developmental disabilities were more likely to earn high wages and be fully integrated in the typical workplace when coworkers were educated about supporting people with disabilities, and there was a good match between the work and the individual's unique talents (Odom et al., 2007). Jobs that are highly predictable, structured, and routine serve this population well (VanBergeijk et al., 2008).

Despite progress in the area of employment noted in the research, unemployment rates for those with disabilities remained near 75% in the 2000's, and those that were employed were more likely to work only part-time with no benefits, and earn a poor wage (Taylor & Seltzer, 2011; Odom et al., 2007). The recent economic downturn has most likely resulted in further decreased employment opportunities for individuals with autism spectrum disorders (Taylor & Seltzer, 2011). Results of the study by Taylor and Seltzer (2011) indicated there may be a group of individuals with autism particularly at risk for poor outcome following the transition to adulthood. They identified a subgroup (25%) of young adults with autism spectrum disorder without intellectual disability who were three times more likely to have no day activities compared to youths with autism spectrum disorder who also had intellectual disability (Taylor & Seltzer, 2011).

There are some predictors of work in the population of individuals with autism spectrum disorders. A study by Holwerda, van der Klink, Groothoff & Brouer (2012) noted that males with autism spectrum disorder are more likely to be employed, as are those with IQs greater than 70. Individuals with co-morbidity, maladaptive behavior, such as odd, challenging, or ritualistic behavior, or lack of empathy are less likely to be employed (Holwerda et al., 2012). The capacity of an individual to complete some self-care skills independently, along with social competence and parental expectations, were considered strong predictors of working after high school (Carter, Austin & Trainor, 2011). Carter et al. (2012) examined student, family, and school factors associated with sustained employment two years after completing high school as they pertain to young adults with severe disabilities defined as intellectual disability, multiple disabilities, or autism. Results indicated that of the 450 students enrolled in the study, 26% were working two years after completion of high school. Paid work experiences during high school were strongly associated with employment during the two years following completion of high school. Students employed during high school made critical connections to local employers and had the potential to raise expectations for participation in the workforce following high school (Carter et al., 2011).

Laws Regarding Individuals with Disabilities in the Workplace

The **Americans with Disabilities Act (ADA)** of 1990 was intended to end discrimination toward individuals with disabilities and promote decent jobs with decent incomes. The ADA also supports the rights of individuals with disabilities within the community, and one year after it was adopted, a comprehensive set of regulations was published that provided for the following: accessibility, non-discrimination, and greater access to workplaces, community facilities, public transportation, and telecommunications (Odom et al., 2007).

The ADA prohibits any public institution from discriminating against individuals with disabilities, and universities need to provide social and academic supports to students with disabilities in order to be in compliance with the ADA (VanBergeijk et al., 2008).

There has been other legislature passed such as **The Rehabilitation Act (Rehab Act)** of 1973. With amendments in 1998, the Rehab Act provides the primary employment support resources for individuals with disabilities. The Rehab Act emphasizes community-integrated employment and provides for matching of federal dollars by state dollars to allow persons with developmental disabilities the opportunity to obtain employment and independent living assistance as needed (Odom et al., 2007).

The **Workforce Investment Act** of 1998 requires states and localities to provide and include appropriate accommodations for those with disabilities, and the **Developmental Disabilities Assistance and Bill of Rights Act** of 2000 established national policy related to those with disabilities characterized by independence, productivity and integration (Odom et al., 2007). People with disabilities who were able to work in the past risked the possibility of losing their Medicare or Medicaid benefits prior to the passage of the **Ticket to Work and Workforce Incentives Improvement Act** of 1999 (Odom et al., 2007).

Quality of Life and Relationships

Despite efforts by lawmakers to improve outcomes for individuals with developmental disabilities, there continue to be many challenges in obtaining a positive quality of life (Howlin et al., 2004). Howlin et al. (2004) found that the majority of individuals diagnosed with autism as children were dependent upon their families and were socially isolated, unable to transition fully to an adult life that included employment, personal relationships and independent living. Another study of 235 adolescents and adults with autism, ages 10-47 years, focused on peer relationships and social and recreational activities (Orsmond, Krauss & Seltzer, 2004). Most study participants (46.4%) had no peer relationships. Only 8.1% of the individuals in the sample reported having a friendship that met criteria including same age, mutual responsiveness, and participation in reciprocal activities outside of organized settings (Orsmond et al., 2004). 38% of the study group engaged in regular group recreational activities, and 30.6 % attended religious services. The group was more likely to participate in those activities if the mother reported her participation as well, and researchers suggested that the mother and individual may be participating in these activities together (Orsmond et al., 2004).

Orsmond et al. (2004) were careful to point out that researchers are not sure that individuals with autism desire friendships, but previous research has indicated high levels of loneliness and lower quality of friendships (Bauminger & Kasari, 2000). Of particular concern are the findings of a study by Shtayerman (2007), who found that adolescents and young adults with Asperger's Syndrome experienced increased levels of peer victimization and suicidal ideation, along with Major Depressive Disorder and Generalized Anxiety Disorder. We need to work hard to ensure that our children and young adults with autism feel connected and see themselves as members of the community.

Strategies to Improve Quality of Life

As we assist students with the transition from school to adult life, there are some intervention strategies that may increase independence and improve outcome. Unfortunately, research in this area is lacking. Individuals with autism spectrum disorders tend to have difficulties with initiation, prompt dependence, and have poor generalization of skills (Hume, Loftin & Lantz, 2009). Other characteristics associated with autism spectrum disorders include problems with joint attention and imitation, which can lead to difficulty watching others in an effort to learn a new skill (Hume et al., 2009). Difficulties with executive function, such as problem-solving through planning, are also common in individuals with autism spectrum disorders. Hume et al. (2009) suggest the use of three specific interventions associated with improving independence:

- **Self-monitoring**: An individual is taught to discriminate and make a record of the occurrence of a target behavior.
- **Video modeling**: Video recordings are made of role-play scenarios involving target skills for the individual to watch as often as needed to acquire the skill.
- **Individual work systems**: A visually organized space where students independently practice skills that have been previously mastered under direct supervision of an adult.

Preparation must be undertaken to address social skill deficits that are commonly seen in individuals with autism. For example, individuals with autism are at a disadvantage when participating in interviews. VanBergeijk et al. (2008) suggest that students be taught how to conduct themselves during interviews by role-playing, practicing a variety of scenarios in reference to introducing themselves, making small talk, determining whether to shake someone's hand, and determining where to sit.

With appropriate support and intervention, individuals with autism spectrum disorders can fulfill their aspirations to become independent contributing members of society (VanBergeijk et al., 2008).

Chapter 6:

Resources

The Autism Society of America

The Autism Society, the nation's leading grassroots autism organization, exists to improve the lives of all affected by autism. They do this by increasing public awareness about the day-to-day issues faced by people on the spectrum, advocating for appropriate services for individuals across the lifespan, and providing the latest information regarding treatment, education, research, and advocacy.

Address: 4340 East-West Highway, Suite 350

Bethesda, MD 20814

Phone: 1-800-328-8476

Website: www.autismsociety.org

Autism Speaks

Autism Speaks was founded in February 2005 by Bob and Suzanne Wright, the grandparents of a child with autism. Autism Speaks has grown into one of the world's leading autism science and advocacy organizations, dedicated to funding research into the causes, prevention, treatments and a cure for autism; increasing awareness of autism spectrum disorders; and advocating for the needs of individuals with autism and their families. Autism Response Team (ART) members are specially trained to connect families with information, resources, and opportunities.

Phone: (888) 288-4762

En Español: (888) 772-9050

Email: familyservices@autismspeaks.org

Website: www.autismspeaks.org

Best Buddies®

Best Buddies® is a nonprofit 501(c)(3) organization dedicated to establishing a global volunteer movement that creates opportunities for one-to-one friendships, integrated employment, and leadership development for people with intellectual and developmental disabilities (IDD).
Founded in 1989 by Anthony K. Shriver, Best Buddies is a vibrant, international organization that has grown from one original chapter to almost 1,700 middle school, high school, and college chapters worldwide.

Best Buddies programs engage participants in each of the 50 United States, and in 50 countries around the world. Best Buddies' eight formal programs — *Middle Schools, High Schools, Colleges, Citizens, e-Buddies®, Jobs, Ambassadors*, and *Promoters* — positively impact nearly 800,000 individuals with and without disabilities worldwide. As a result of their involvement with Best Buddies, people with IDD secure rewarding jobs, live on their own, become inspirational leaders, and make lifelong friendships. Although Best Buddies has advanced tremendously in its short existence, many areas of the country and many regions of the world still lack programs to help people with IDD become part of mainstream society. With that in mind, Best Buddies is systematically implementing its 2020 Initiative, which will witness the organization's continued significant growth, both domestically and overseas.

Best Buddies Global Headquarters

Address:	100 Southeast Second Street, Suite 2200
	Miami, FL 33131
Phone:	(305) 374-2233
Toll Free:	(800) 89-BUDDY (28339)
Website:	bestbuddies.org

National Autism Association

The mission of the National Autism Association is to respond to the most urgent needs of the autism community, providing real help and hope so that all affected can reach their full potential.

Address:	One Park Avenue, Suite 1
	Portsmouth, RI 0287
Phone:	(877) 622- 2884
Website:	nationalautismassociation.org

Resources for Feeding Difficulties:

Feeding Matters

Parents can obtain valuable information from Feeding Matters at www.feedingmatters.org. This organization is committed to conquering pediatric feeding struggles and provides education, resources and support to families and medical professionals.

The American Speech-Language Hearing Association, at www.asha.org, is another source of information about feeding disorders and additional resources that may be of benefit to parents and professionals.

The National Foundation of Swallowing Disorders provides information and support to those affected by dysphagia.

Parents can obtain information at www.swallowingdisorder-foundation.com.

Siblings

Autism Speaks

As referenced above, this organization provides online information and "toolkits for family support," including "A sibling's guide to autism." They may be found online at www.autismspeaks.org.

Books for Siblings, as recommended by Autism Speaks:

The Autism Acceptance Book: Being a Friend to Someone with Autism
by Ellen Sabin

My Brother Charlie
by Holly Robinson Peete and Ryan Elizabeth Peete

Leah's Voice
By Lori DeMonia

The Other Kid (interactive workbook available in English and Spanish)
by Lorraine Donlon (www.theotherkid.com)

Siblings: The Autism Spectrum Through Our Eyes
by Jane Johnson and Anne Van Rensselaer

Sibshops: Workshops for Siblings of Children with Special Needs
by Donald J. Meyer and Patricia F. Vadasy

Sometimes My Brother: Helping Kids Understand Autism Through a Sibling's Eyes
by Angie Healy

Sibling Support Group

The Sibling Support Project is a national effort dedicated

to the lifelong concerns of brothers and sisters of people who have special health, developmental, or mental health concerns.

Website: www.siblingsupport.org

Grandparents

Autism Speaks

As referenced above, this organization provides online information and "toolkits for family support," including grandparents. They may be found online at www.autismspeaks.org.

Books for grandparents, as recommended by Autism Speaks:

Grandparenting A Child with Special Needs
by Charlotte E. Thompson, MD

The Grandparent Connection
by Jennifer Krumins

Letters to Sam: A Grandfather's Lessons on Love, Loss, and the Gifts of Life
by Daniel Gottlieb

A Practical Guide to Autism: What Every Parent, Family Member and Teacher Needs to Know
by Fred R. Volkmar

Grandparent Support Group:
www.orgsites.com/fl/autismgrandparents

Grandparent Autism Network: www.ganinfo.org

References

American Psychiatric Association. (2013). *Diagnostic and Statistical Manual of Mental Disorders* (5 ed.). Arlington, VA: American Psychiatric Publishing.

National Dissemination Center for Children with Disabilities. (n.d.). *Overview of early intervention*. Retrieved 2013, from nichcy.org: http://nichcy.org/babies/overview

Barnhill, G., Hagiwara, T., Myles, B., & Simpson, R. (2000). Asperger syndrome: a study of the cognitive profiles of 37 children and adolescents. *Focus on Autism and Other Developmental Disabilities*, 146-153.

Bauminger, N. & Kasari, C. (2000). Loneliness and friendship in high-functioning children with autism. *Child Development*, 447-456.

Boyd, B., Odom, S., Humphreys, B., & Sam, A. (2010). Infants and toddlers with autism spectrum disorder: early identification and early intervention. *Journal of Early Intervention*, 75-98.

Brown, I. & Percy, M. (2007). *A Comprehensive Guide to Intellectual and Developmental Disabilities.* Baltimore: Paul H. Brookes Publishing Company.

Carter, E., Austin, D. & Trainor, A. (2011). Predictors of postschool employment outcomes for young adults with severe disabilities. *Journal of Disability Policy Studies*. doi:10.1177/1044207311414680

Center for Disease Control. (2014, March 24). Retrieved on September 5, 2014, from http://www.cdc.gov/ncbdd/autism/data.html

Chamberlain, B., Kasari, C., & Rotheram-Fuller, E. (2007). Involvement or isolation? The social networks of children with autism in regular classrooms. *Journal of Autism and Developmental Disorders*, 230-242. doi:10.1007/s10803-006-0164-4

Charman, T. & Baird, G. (2002). Practitioner Review: diagnosis of autism spectrum disorder in 2- and 3- year old children. *Journal of Child Psychology and Psychiatry*, 289-305.

Corsello, C. (2005). Early intervention in autism. *Infants & Young Children*, 74-85.

Crosland, K. & Dunlap, G. (2012). Effective strategies for the inclusion of children with autism in general education classrooms. *Behavior Modification*, 251-269. doi:10.1177/0145445512442682

Dahle, K. (2003). Services to include young children with autism in the general classroom. *Early Childhood Education Journal*, 65-70. doi:10.1023/A:1025193020415

Dawson, G. (2008). Early behavioral intervention, brain plasticity, and the prevention of autism spectrum disorder. *Developmental Psychopathology*, 775-803.

Dawson, G. R. (2009). Randomized, controlled trial of an intervention for toddlers with autism: The Early Start Denver Model. *Pediatrics*, e17-e23.

Diagnostic and Statistical Manual of Mental Disorders. (2000). Washington DC: American Psychiatric Association.

Eldevik, S., Hastings, R., Hughes, C., Jahr, E., Eikeseth, S., & Cross, S. (2009). Meta-analysis of early intensive behavioral intervention for children with autism. *Journal of Clinical Child & Adolescent Psychology*, 439-450.

Florida Inclusion Network. (n.d.). Retrieved February 17, 2013, from www.FloridaInclusionNetwork: www.FloridaInclusionNetwork

Fombonne, E; In Volkmar, F., Paul, R., Klin, A. & Cohen, D. (2005). Epidemiological studies of pervasive developmental disorders. *Handbook of autism and pervasive developmental disorders, 3rd ed.*

Gardner, J. & Chapman, M. (1993). *Developing Staff Competencies for Supporting People with Developmental Disabilities.* Baltimore: Paul H. Brookes Publishing Company.

Guralnick, M. (1998). Effectiveness of early intervention for vulnerable children: A developmental perspective. *American Journal on Mental Retardation*, 319-345.

Hanson, M. & Lynch, E. (2004). *Understanding families: approaches to diversity, disability and risk.* Baltimore: Paul H. Brookes Publishing Co.

Harrower, J. & Dunlap, G. (2001). Including children with autism in general education classrooms. *Behavior Modification*, 762-784.

Hebbler, K. (2007). *Early intervention for infants and toddlers with disabilities and their families: Participants, services and outcomes: Final report of the National Early Intervention Longitudinal Study (NEILS).* Menlo Park, CA: Stanford Research Institute.

Hillman, J. (2007). Grandparents of children with autism: a review with recommendations for education, practice and policy. *Educational Gerontology*, 513-527.

Holwerda, A., van der Klink, J., Groothoff, J. & Brouwer, S. (2012). Predictors for work participation in individuals with an autism spectrum disorder: a systematic review. *Journal of Occupational Rehabilitation*, 333-352.

Howard, P. (2004, April). The least restrictive environment: How to tell? *Journal of Law & Education Act, 33*(2), 167-180.

Howlin, P., Goode, S., Hutton, J. & Rutter, M. (2004). Adult outcomes for children with autism. *Journal of Child Psychology and Psychiatry*, 212-229.

Hume, K., Loftin, R. & Lantz, J. (2009). Increasing independence in autism spectrum disorders: A review of three focused interventions. *Journal of Autism and Developmental Disorders*, 1329-1338.

Irva Hertz-Piccioto, L. A. (2006). The CHARGE study: An epidemiologic investigation of genetic and environmental factors contibuting to autism. *Environmental Health Perspectives*, 1119-1125.

Logan, K. & Keefe, E. . (1997). A comparison of instructional context, teacher behavior, and engaged behavior for students with severe disabilities in general education and self-contained elementary classrooms. *Journal of the Association for Persons with Severe Handicaps*, 16-27.

Mandell, D. & Salzer, M. (2007). Who joins support groups amonth parents of children with autism? *Autism*, 111-122. doi:10.1177/1362361307077506

Mundy, P. & Newell, L. (2007). Attention, joint attention, and social cognition. *Current Directions in Psychological Science*, 269-274. doi:10.1111/j.1467-8721.2007.00518.x.

National Dissemination Center for Children with Disabilities. (n.d.). *Overview of early intervention.* Retrieved 2013, from nichcy.org: http://nichcy.org/babies/overview

Odom, S., Horner, R., Snell, M. & Blacher, J. (2007). *Handbook of developmental disabilities.* New York, New York: The Guilford Press.

Orsmond, G., Krauss, M. & Seltzer, M. (2004). Peer relationships and social and recreational activities among adolescents and adults with autism. *Journal of Autism and Developmental Disorders*, 245-256.

Osterling, J., Dawson G., & Munson, J. (2002). Early recognition of 1 year old infants with autism spectrum disorder versus mental retardation. *Development and Psychopathology*, 239-251.

Pellicano, E. (2012). Do autistic symptoms persist across time? Evidence of substantial change in symptomatology over a 3 year period in cognitively able children with autism. *American Journal on Intellectual and Developmental Disabilites*, 156-166.

Roberts-Dahm, D. G. (Ed.). (2005). *Transition planning for students with disabilities: A guide for families.* Retrieved March 3, 2013, from Florida Department of Education: http://www.fldoe.org/ese/rtf/Transition-Guide.rtf

Sailor, W., Dunlap, G., Sugai, G., & Horner, R. (2009). *Handbook of positive behavior support.* New York:

Springer.

Sansosti, J. & Sansosti, F. (2012). Inclusion for students with high-functioning autism spectrum disorders: definitions and decision making. *Psychology in the Schools*, 917-931. doi:10.1002/pits.21652

Shtayermman, O. (2007). Peer victimization in the adolescents and young adults diagnosed with Asperger's Syndrome: a link to depressive symptomatology, anxiety symptomatology and suicidal ideation. *Issues in Comprehensive Pediatric Nursing*, 87-107.

Smith, T. (2012). *Making inclusion work for students with autism spectrum disorders: An evidence-based guide.* Guilford Publications. Retrieved February 7, 2013, from <http://lib.mylibrary.com?ID=330603

Tomsho, R. (2007, November 7). Parents of disabled children push for separate classes. *The Wall Street Journal*, A1.

Webster's Dictionary for Students. (2003). Springfield, MA: Federal Street Press.

Williams, P., Piamjariyakul, U., Graff, J., & Stanton, A. (2010). Developmental disabilities: Effects on well siblings . *Issues in Comprehensive Pediatric nursing*, 39-55.

Williams, P., Ridder, L., Setter, R., Liebergen, A., Curry, H., Piamjariyakul, U., & Williams, A. (2009). Pediatric chronic illness effects on well siblings: parents' voices. *Issues in Comprehensive Pediatric Nursing*, 94-113.

Winzer, M. (2002). *Children with exceptionalities in Canadian classrooms.* Toronto: Prentice Hall.

Made in the USA
Monee, IL
04 November 2026

67386415R00039